Rosie, A Detroit Herstory

Great Lakes Books

A complete listing of the books in this series can be found online at
wsupress.wayne.edu

ROSIE
A Detroit Herstory

Bailey Sisoy Isgro

Illustrated by Nicole Lapointe

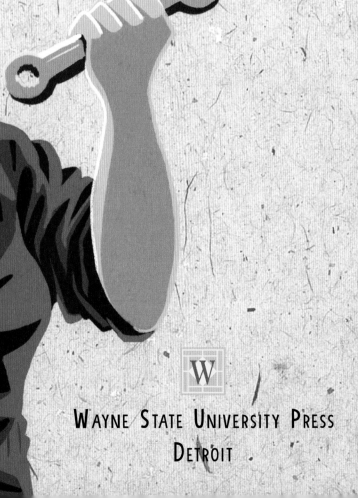

WAYNE STATE UNIVERSITY PRESS

DETROIT

ISBN: 978-0-8143-4544-3 (hardcover); 978-0-8143-4545-0 (ebook)

Library of Congress Control Number: 2018944526

Wayne State University Press
Leonard N. Simons Building
4809 Woodward Avenue
Detroit, Michigan 48201–1309

Visit us online at wsupress.wayne.edu

For Mom and Gram, who
made sure I loved books,
history, and Detroit.

WORLD WAR II

In 1939, World War II exploded across Europe when the chancellor of Germany, Adolf Hitler, and his Nazi party commanded the German army to invade the nearby country of Poland.

As Germany teamed up with Italy and Japan to form the "Axis powers" and spread their rule across the globe, nineteen nations rose in opposition from North America, Europe, and Asia. These countries—led by England, the United States of America, the Soviet Union, and China—would become the "Allied powers."

U.S. President Franklin Delano Roosevelt was pressured by prominent businessmen, celebrities, and politicians to keep America out of the war. They believed that America should come first, and that the vast oceans separated the U.S. from a war halfway around the world.

As allies like England's Prime Minister Winston Churchill pleaded for help, President Roosevelt made an impassioned argument: "Suppose my neighbor's home catches fire, and I have a length of garden hose four or five hundred feet away. If he can take my garden hose and connect it up with his hydrant, I may help him to put out his fire. . . . I don't say

to him before that operation, 'Neighbor, my garden hose cost me $15; you have to pay me $15 for it.'. . . I don't want $15—I want my garden hose back after the fire is over."

What President Roosevelt didn't realize was how much of that help would come from two unlikely sources—the city of Detroit and a generation of tough, industrious women we call "Rosies."

WOMEN AT WAR

During World War II, women worked in every imaginable field, doing jobs that were previously the exclusive domain of men.

From running family businesses to managing farms, from operating machinery to working on the assembly line, women stepped into the gaps left by men marching off to war. All across America, women produced ships, tanks, ammunition, uniforms, jeeps, and planes in spectacular quantities.

No industry was more greatly affected by this change than aviation and aircraft production, particularly at facilities like Michigan's influential Willow Run Plant. Over 310,000 women worked in the U.S. aircraft industry in 1943, making up 65 percent of the industry's workforce—an astonishing number compared to 1940, when women represented just 1 percent.

Whether for reasons economic or patriotic—or to simply capitalize on newfound workplace opportunities—women entered the workforce in never-before-seen numbers during the war. Their skill, bravery, tenacity, and spirit became a rallying point of American patriotism and supplied America's Allies with some much-needed manufacturing might.

However, while women workers were invaluable to the war effort, their salaries, job security, personal safety, and overall treatment quite often lagged behind those of their male counterparts. Female workers rarely earned more than 50 percent of what men earned, were routinely laid off before men, and were often subjected to harsh treatment because of their gender.

Yet, for all their struggles, their successes were monumental.

Today, we know them as Rosies, a group of women defined not by the identity of a single riveter in a single factory but by the collective might of hundreds of thousands of women whose labors helped save the world.

To all of the Rosies—thank you for everything!

A world war and a president's decree
Began a quest in which women were key.
Heroines emerged that no one expected,
Young women building the unprecedented.

Across America, women showed their might.
Rosie the Riveter was born in this fight.
And, in Detroit, where battles never waged,
They helped win a war and saw a nation changed.

This true story starts before most women had careers,
And a world war occupied nearly everyone's fears . . .

In September nineteen hundred and thirty-nine,
The Germans crossed over Poland's territory line.
"The Nazis invaded, we have to help out!"
Yelled President Roosevelt without any doubt.

But, as England and France both entered the fight,
Americans suffered from nearness of sight.
"Our oceans protect us, we're so far away!"
Their isolationism no one could sway.

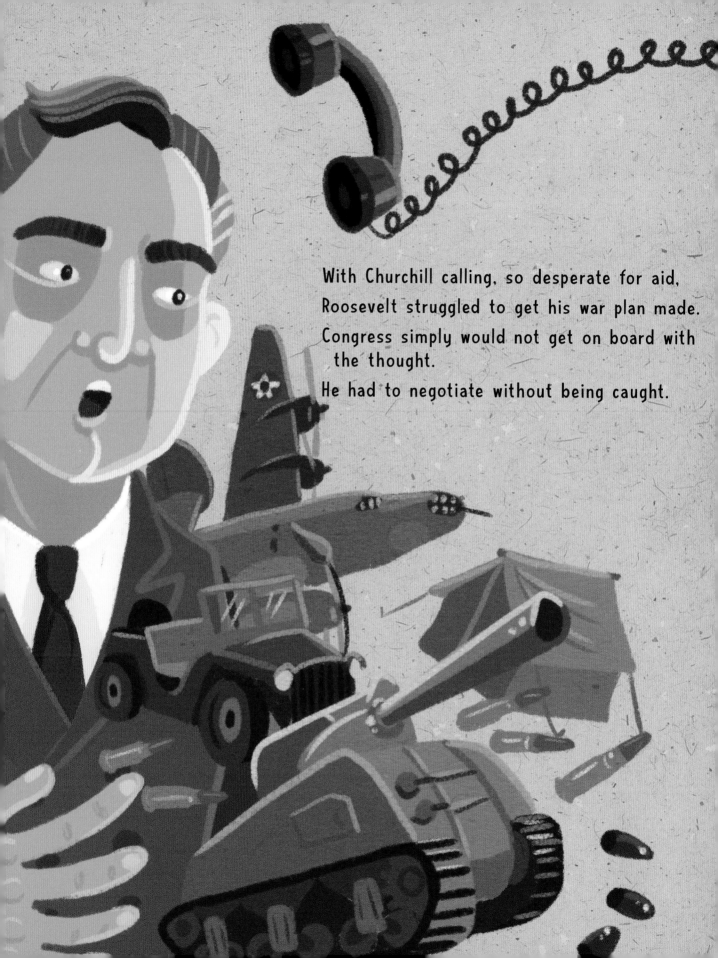

With Churchill calling, so desperate for aid,
Roosevelt struggled to get his war plan made.
Congress simply would not get on board with
  the thought.
He had to negotiate without being caught.

In back rooms, there was born a political deal.

"We'll trade boats and airplanes for a real estate steal."

With that quite clever scheme, Lend-Lease was enacted.

Now U.S. war material could be crafted.

Foundations for airplane factories
were laid.

Their production increased, more and
more were made.

As the newspapers published
frightening war scoops,

Congress still refused to send
American troops.

"Oh, the German Luftwaffe can never be caught!"
"Building planes means workers who'll have to be taught!"
But Detroit answered back with a resounding cry,
"We'll all do our very best! We'll try and we'll try!"

Detroit knew how to build and how to build fast,
With knowledge of machinery that was vast.
To build equipment at never-before-seen speed,
The auto industry needed to take the lead.

Lend-Lease ensured the Allies were not overrun,
Until a sad surprise in nineteen forty-one.

On December seventh, early in the morning,
Pearl Harbor was ambushed without any warning.
Hundreds of airplanes led the Axis attack.
The U.S. Navy was left battered and cracked.

World War II was declared, and everything changed.
A nationwide war draft was quickly arranged.

Off to the war, the men of Detroit soon marched.
At home, blue coveralls were ironed and starched.
Bandannas were tied around victory curls
By new factory workers—women and girls.

From family bars to the Mom and Pop shops,
Women took over the jobs, managed the crops.
Ladies kept the lights on and the "Open" signs hung,
Running businesses while the men were far-flung.

Bright-eyed women were plucked from local high schools
And automotive secretarial pools.
They were tested for aptitude, measured, and weighed,
Sent off to training class without being delayed.

Now that the fires of war and industry were lit,
The women of Detroit declared, "We can do it!"

The women's brave reputation began to expand,
So songwriters teamed up with the Kay Kyser band.
The group wrote a hit song that coined the women's name,
Catapulting their war efforts to global fame.

Bestowed with a nickname that's still with us today,
"Rosie the Riveter" earned her factory pay.

Top brass needed a place to oversee all,
Somewhere in Detroit, something big and quite tall.
The Guardian Building gave renter reduction,
Becoming a center of wartime production.

From the Art Deco building, orders were spitting,
As all normal auto production was quitting.
Not a single civilian car would be made
Until the war ended with a victor's parade.

From Liberator bombers to Sherman tanks,
Massive battleships to machine gunner cranks,
Bullets by the millions and bombs by the ton,
The women of Detroit helped get it all done!

With a welding torch and a riveting gun,
Rosies invented new ways to get the work done.
Women retrieved parts quickly on roller skates,
They used pulleys and gears to stack heavy crates.

The smallest would climb inside the airplane wings,
Attaching the rudder, steering, and flap strings.
They worked all-night shifts without saying a word,
Even while practice air raid sirens were heard.

Now off the Highland Park Ford Factory floor,
Rolled the Rolls Royce engines that made the planes soar.

Shipped to assembly at a new Ford endeavor—
Willow Run, the world's largest factory ever!

"A bomber an hour!" was Willow Run's goal,
As the Rosies worked hard, with heart and with soul.
The Ladies Air Core was the best of the best,
Putting B-24s through every flight test.

Rosie's image graced the *Saturday Evening Post*,
Painted by Norman Rockwell and seen coast to coast.
Women War Workers each had their own unique name,
But, thanks to strong Rosie, their labors found fame.

Rosie's Women War Workers were an exciting new breed.
"On her, their lives depend" was Rosie's solemn creed.

Her efforts kept the hopes of the Allies alive
Until one fateful day in nineteen forty-five.
May eighth brought Germany's unconditional surrender
After millions of man-hours, regardless of gender.

Many lives were shattered, losses deeply felt.
Across the world, families grieved and they knelt.
But among the great heroes who won World War II
Were Rosie's War Workers whose legend only grew.

Troops returned to Detroit through the train station,
Men excited to come back to their home nation.
But now the Rosies who built all the planes and warships
Were fired from factories and handed pink slips.
Women found that as soon as the men had returned
Their manufacturing knowledge seemed to be spurned.

Some women were eager for a regular pace,
Others wanted to get right back into the workplace.
They'd spent four long years, earning their own paychecks,
And could not accept they were now the wrong sex.

Today when you walk onto a factory floor,
You will find more women than ever before.
Because, deep in the souls and the hearts of each one,
Rests the enduring victory all Rosies won.

Women working at the Chrysler DeSoto Plant, August 1, 1942. Walter P. Reuther Library, Archives of Labor and Urban Affairs, Wayne State University.

TIME LINE

January 30, 1933

Adolf Hitler becomes chancellor of Germany.

May 1, 1937

U.S. President Franklin D. Roosevelt signs the 1937 Neutrality Act, in an effort to distance the United States from growing political conflicts in Europe and Asia.

September 1, 1939

German troops march over the border into Poland. This act of aggression officially begins what becomes World War II.

September 3, 1939

Britain and France declare war on Germany, in response to the Polish invasion. President Roosevelt invokes the Neutrality Act but notes, "Even a neutral cannot be asked to close his mind or his conscience."

August 1940

Before the U.S. officially joins the war effort, Congress appropriates $16 billion for defense needs and enacts the first peacetime draft in American history. During World War II, 613,543 Michiganders would go on to serve in the United States armed services.

September 1940

The America First Committee (AFC) forms. It was the largest group in the United States devoted to keeping the country from entering World War II. Among its members were Henry Ford, aviator Charles Lindbergh, novelist Sinclair Lewis, poet E. E. Cummings, Walt Disney, actress Lillian Gish, and architect Frank Lloyd Wright. Members of the AFC were called "Isolationists" and believed that America's geographic location would keep it safe from attacks.

September 27, 1940

Germany, Japan, and Italy sign the Tripartite Pact in Berlin. The three nations formally become known as the "Axis powers."

October 1940

K. T. Keller, president of Chrysler Corporation, is placed in charge of the yet-to-be-built tank arsenal in Warren, Michigan. The Tank Automotive Center—responsible for "the design, production, delivery, and servicing" of every vehicle in the military—is moved from Washington, D.C., to the Union Guardian Building in Detroit.

October 29, 1940

The first U.S. draft numbers are drawn, sending thousands of male American draftees to military drill camps throughout the country, where they would become trained to be soldiers. In response, women begin to fill the gaps left in the labor market.

November 1940

Roosevelt is elected for his third term as U.S. president.

December 29, 1940

In an address to the United States, President Roosevelt announces, "We must be the great Arsenal of Democracy."

January 6, 1941

Before the U.S. Congress, President Roosevelt proposes the Lend-Lease Act, which is formally titled "An Act to Promote the Defense of the United States." It supplies France, the United Kingdom, the Republic of China, and the Soviet Union, along with other Allied nations, with necessary war material. Congress goes on to approve the bill.

December 7, 1941

Japanese fighter planes attack the American military base at Pearl Harbor, Hawaii, destroying many U.S. aircraft and naval vessels and killing 2,355 U.S. servicemen and 68 civilians.

December 10, 1941

The America First Committee is dissolved.

December 11, 1941

Germany and Italy declare war on the United States. The United States declares war on Germany, Italy, and Japan.

1942

The term "Rosie the Riveter" is first used in a song titled "Rosie the Riveter," written by Redd Evans and John Jacob Loeb. The song is recorded by the renowned big-band leader James Kern "Kay" Kyser and becomes a national hit.

January 1942

Artist J. Howard Miller is hired by the Westinghouse Company's War Production Coordinating Committee to paint a series of war effort posters. Among his creations is the iconic "We Can Do It!" image. Although the image would later be called "Rosie the Riveter," it wasn't actually given that title until after World War II.

January 6, 1942

President Roosevelt delivers his State of the Union address in which he proposes a massive government spending budget. It will be the largest budget in American history, with huge sums going to Detroit manufacturing for the war effort.

July 21, 1942

The United States Naval Reserve (Women's Reserve)—better known as W.A.V.E.S. (Women Accepted for Volunteer Emergency Service)—is founded.

August 1942

The Willow Run Factory in Ypsilanti, Michigan, opens. It was the largest factory under one roof in the world, at 3 million square feet in size, with two assembly lines more than a mile long each. It earns the nickname "Will It Run" as the factory is plagued with problems after opening.

August 18, 1942

The U.S. Office of Price Administration bans the sale of new cars to non-military personnel. In Detroit, production of war material increases as civilian production stops. More and more women flood into the war effort.

1942 to 1945

Michigan companies produce 4 million engines and 200,000 cars and trucks during the war. Detroit—a city with 2 percent of the U.S. population at the time—made 10 percent of the material supplies for World War II. Ford Motor Company made over 8,500 B-24 Liberator bombers at Willow Run, and Chrysler produced over 25,000 tanks.

May 29, 1943

Norman Rockwell's famous *Saturday Evening Post* cover "Rosie the Riveter" hits newsstands.

August 1943

The Willow Run Factory begins mass production with the eventual goal of a bomber an hour. Willow Run employs 42,000 workers; one-third are women.

September 8, 1943

Following defeats across Europe and Africa, the Italian government officially surrenders to the Allied powers.

June 6, 1944

Known as D-Day, this Allied attack is one of the largest military operations in history. Nearly 3 million Allied soldiers storm the beaches of Normandy, on the northern shores of France. After looking out at all the ships and planes involved in the attack, an American radio operator later commented that "obviously Rosie the Riveter back home had been very busy."

April 12, 1945

President Franklin D. Roosevelt dies.

April 30, 1945

Adolf Hitler dies by suicide.

May 2, 1945

The German army signs an unconditional surrender. The war in Europe ends, though the war against Japan and the Allied forces in the Pacific Ocean still continues.

May 1945

The demobilization of the American army begins as soldiers, sailors, and airmen are sent home from the European front. Orders for war material slow as victory in the Pacific seems more and more likely.

June 28, 1945

The last B-24 bomber rolls off the line at the Willow Run Factory—it was number 8,685.

September 2, 1945

World War II officially ends with Japan's unconditional surrender. A formal surrender ceremony is conducted in Tokyo Bay on the USS *Missouri*.

March 10, 2010

Nearly seventy years after they were disbanded, the Women Airforce Service Pilots (WASPs) receive the Congressional Gold Medal, the highest civilian honor bestowed by Congress. During World War II, 350,000 women served in the U.S. armed forces, both at home and abroad. They included the civilian Women's Airforce Service Pilots, some of whom served as test pilots at the Willow Run Factory.

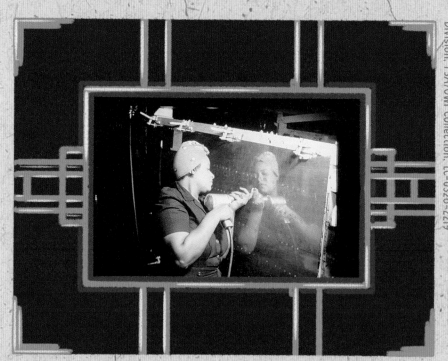

Operating a hand drill at the Vultee Plant in Nashville, Tennessee, a woman works on a Vengeance dive bomber.

October 24, 2015

2,096 women dressed as Rosie the Riveter descend on the historic Willow Run Factory and claim the Guinness World Record for the greatest number of "Tribute Rosies."

October 14, 2017

After enjoying a good-natured battle for the record with a California "Rosie" group, 3,755 women once again don their coveralls and bandannas to bring the record back home to Michigan. As the Guinness World Record committee declares the victory, a roar of success rises from the crowd. From the aging women who originally worked in the wartime factories to the newborn babies in their mothers' arms—each and every one is dressed as Rosie.

Women moving a huge tail section onto a bomber production line at the Willow Run Plant. Production of Consolidated B-24 Liberators, August 2, 1943. Walter P. Reuther Library, Archives of Labor and Urban Affairs, Wayne State University.

Women at the Chrysler DeSoto Plant, August 1, 1942. Walter P. Reuther Library, Archives of Labor and Urban Affairs, Wayne State University.

WORDS TO KNOW

Allied Forces: The name given to the 26 nations that opposed the Axis powers during World War II. The Allied Forces were led by their three largest and richest countries: the United Kingdom, the Soviet Union, and the United States.

Art Deco: The predominant architectural style of the 1920s and 1930s. Many of Detroit's buildings were built in this style, which is characterized by bold geometric shapes and strong colors.

Axis Powers: The name given to the nations of Germany, Italy, and Japan, which joined forces to expand their global power during World War II.

Congress: A governing body of the federal government of the United States. It is made up of two houses: the Senate and the House of Representatives. In the United States, only Congress has the power to declare war, not the president.

Draft: Legally mandated military service that provides the armed forces with soldiers, sailors, and other military personnel. The draft—also known as conscription—is used during times of war when volunteer enlistment is not sufficient enough to meet military needs. During World War II, around 20 percent of the military was drafted into service.

Franklin Delano Roosevelt: The thirty-second president of the United States of America. He was in office for most of World War II, serving from 1932 until his death in 1945. He worked with Winston Churchill to create the Lend-Lease program.

Isolationist: A nation, person, or government that withdraws from world affairs. During World War II, America refrained from entering the war largely because of Isolationist ideals that argued a European war didn't need to be an American war. Famous American isolationists included Walt Disney, Charles Lindbergh, and Henry Ford.

Lend-Lease: A plan devised by President Roosevelt in 1941 that allowed the United States to build and supply military equipment, transport vehicles, and ammunition to the United Kingdom and its allies, without officially declaring war. The plan was designed as a loan program where the U.S. was traded British-owned military bases in exchange for war materials.

Liberator B-24 Bomber: An American-designed and American-made heavy bomber airplane. It was designed by Consolidated Aircraft of San Diego, California, and built in several factories—none more famously than Michigan's Willow Run Plant, which produced more than 8,600 of them during World War II.

Luftwaffe: Nazi Germany's Air Force. The Luftwaffe was the aerial branch of Hitler's armed forces. It was thought to be unbeatable until the Allies benefited from the mass production of American warplanes like the B-24 Liberator.

Nazi: Members of the National Socialist German Workers' Party, a political party that came to power in Germany in 1919 under Adolf Hitler. The Nazi party believed they were superior to all other races and practiced ethnic cleansing—the killing of an entire group of people because they share a religion or culture that is found undesirable. The Nazis murdered millions of people during World War II because of their nationalities, religions, political beliefs, and sexual orientations.

Riveter: A person who operates a riveting gun, which works like a stapler for metal. By punching or drilling a hole through two or more pieces of metal, a riveter joins the pieces together by flattening them out and driving a rivet—a special fastener—through the new hole. Sometimes riveters work in teams while fastening together larger pieces of metal—like on an airplane—and sometimes they work alone on smaller parts.

Saturday Evening Post: One of America's most enduring publications. For almost 200 years, the magazine has covered all aspects of American life. It was particularly well-known for its iconic covers painted by American artist Norman Rockwell, which are still prized by art collectors today.

Sherman Tanks: The most recognizable American tank of World War II was the M4 Sherman. It was used in both Europe and the Pacific by the U.S. Army and Marine Corps. Under Lend-Lease, it became the most commonly used tank for the other Allied nations as well. Sherman Tanks were largely built in Michigan's Arsenal Tank Plant, just outside of Detroit.

Top Brass: Slang term for the most important military officers and politicians.

Unconditional Surrender: A surrender in which no guarantees (safe travel, prisoner exchange, or restitution) are given to the surrendering party. The Allies demanded what is known as an Unconditional Surrender from the Axis powers.

Willow Run Factory: A factory constructed by the Ford Motor Company in Ypsilanti, Michigan, to mass produce B-24 Liberator Bombers for World War II. It was the largest factory in the world when completed and, against all odds, produced a bomber an hour before the war's end.

Winston Churchill: The prime minister of the United Kingdom during World War II. The prime minister is the elected head of the government in the United Kingdom.

Women's Civilian Air Corps: A civilian women pilots' organization, whose members were United States federal civil service employees. The Women Airforce Service Pilots were known by the acronym WASP and referred to as the Women's Army Service Pilots or the Women's Civilian Air Corps. They handled the test flights for airplanes while male pilots were assigned to battle flights.

World War II: A worldwide war that took place from 1939 to 1945. Although America didn't enter the war until December 1941, eventually, almost every nation on Earth was involved in the conflict. It became the largest war in world history with 30 countries, over 100 million people, and billions of dollars involved. 613,543 Michiganders served in the military during World War II.

New Britain, Connecticut. Women welders at the Landers, Frary, and Clark Plant.

About the Author

Bailey Sisoy Isgro is the owner of Detroit History Tours and the proprietress of the Detroit History Club. She is an author, humorist, workaholic, and Faygo-loving feminist from the great city of Detroit. A lover of city ephemera, her most prized possessions include her antique books about Detroit, her Library of Congress reader's card, and her collection of vintage jewelry. She works as an automotive sculptor by day and by night she writes and lectures on the history of her fine city.

About the Illustrator

Nicole Lapointe is a local Detroit freelance artist and resident geek. She's passionate about Detroit's French heritage and weird folktales. When she's not working on art and commissions in her little shop of horrors (a spooky room in the basement of an 1800s Queen Anne in Detroit's famed Canfield neighborhood), she can be found volunteering around town, dressing up in costumes, biking, and never taking a serious photo. Ever.